ROGER STAUBACH, EMMITT SMITH, DARYL JOHNSTON, MICHAEL IRVIN, BOB HAYES, JASON WITTEN, RAYFIELD WRIGHT, ERIK WILLIAMS, LARRY ALLEN, JOHN NILAND, MARK STEPNOSKI, HARVEY MARTIN, ED "TOO TALL" JONES, RANDY WHITE, BOB LILLY, CHUCK HOWLEY, LEE ROY JORDAN, DEMARCUS WARE, MEL RENFRO, DEION SANDERS, CLIFF HARRIS, DARREN WOODSON, RAFAEL SEPTIEN, MAT MCBRIAR, ROGER STAUBACH, EMMITT SMITH, DARYL JOHNSTON, MICHAEL IRVIN, BOB HAYES, JASON WITTEN, RAYFIELD WRIGHT, ERIK WILLIAMS

THE STORY OF THE DALLAS COWBOYS

THE STORY OF THE
DALLAS COWBOYS

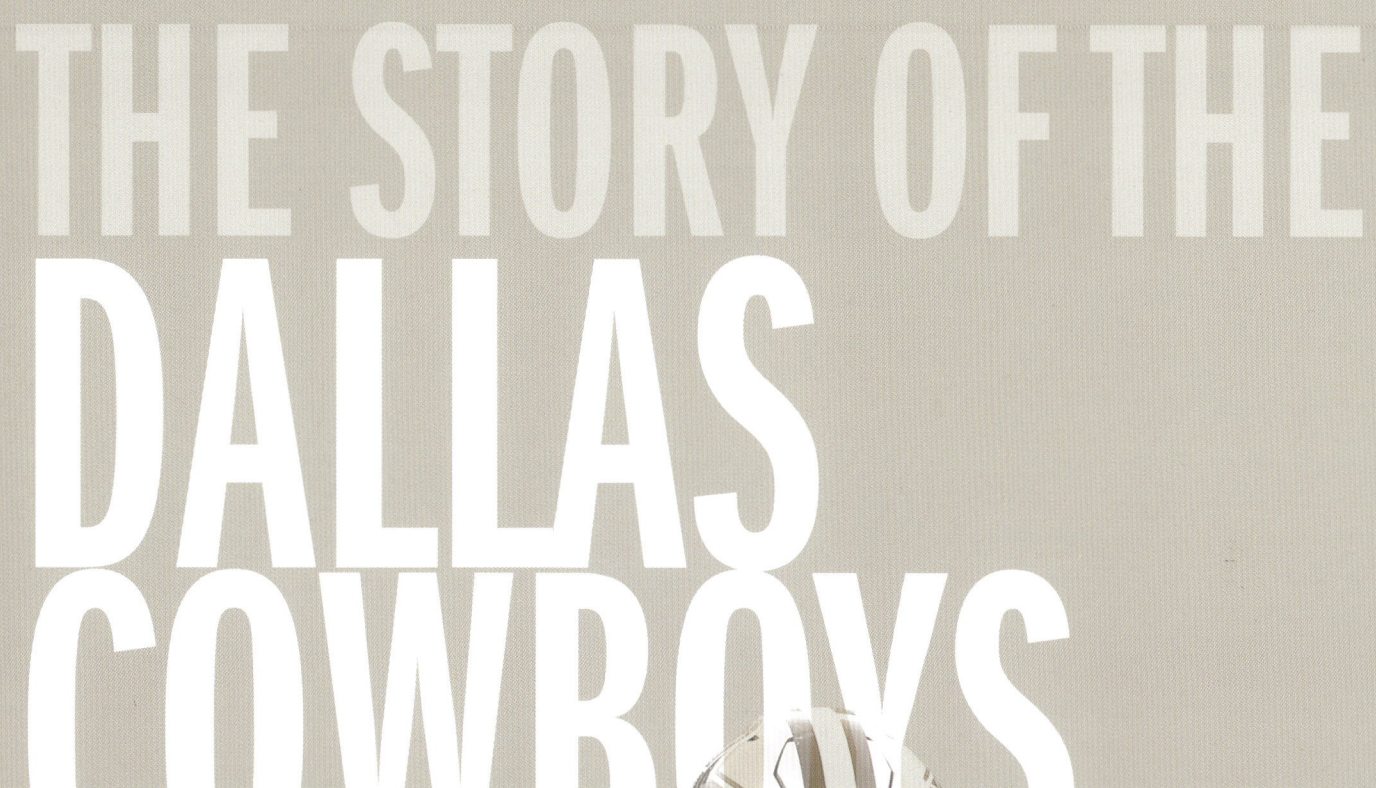

BY JIM WHITING
CREATIVE EDUCATION / CREATIVE PAPERBACKS

Published by Creative Education and Creative Paperbacks
P.O. Box 227, Mankato, Minnesota 56002
Creative Education and Creative Paperbacks are imprints of The Creative Company
www.thecreativecompany.us

Design and production by Blue Design (www.bluedes.com)
Art direction by Rita Marshall
Printed in China

Photographs by AP Images (Associated Press), Corbis (Bettmann), Getty Images (Jonathan Daniel, Diamond Images, James Drake/SI, Nate Fine, Focus on Sport, George Gojkovich, Otto Greule Jr., Grant Halverson, Wesley Hitt, Richard Mackson/SI, Rodger Mallison/Fort Worth Star-Telegram/TNS, Ronald Martinez, Patrick McDermott/Stringer, Jim McIsaac, Ronald C. Modra/Sports Imagery, Tom Pennington, George Rose, Tony Tomsic/NFL, Greg Trott/NFL Photos)

Copyright © 2020 Creative Education, Creative Paperbacks
International copyright reserved in all countries. No part of this book may be reproduced in any form without written permission from the publisher.

Names: Whiting, Jim, author.
Title: The Story of the Dallas Cowboys / Jim Whiting.
Series: NFL Today.
Includes index.
Summary: This high-interest history of the National Football League's Dallas Cowboys highlights memorable games, summarizes seasonal triumphs and defeats, and features standout players such as Emmitt Smith.
Identifiers: LCCN 2018041018 / ISBN 978-1-64026-138-9 (hardcover) / ISBN 978-1-62832-701-4 (pbk) / ISBN 978-1-64000-256-2 (ebook)
Subjects: LCSH: Dallas Cowboys (Football team)—History—Juvenile literature. / Football players—United States—Biography—Juvenile literature.
Classification: LCC GV956.D3 W44 2019 / DDC 796.332/64097642812—DC23

First Edition HC 9 8 7 6 5 4 3 2 1
First Edition PBK 9 8 7 6 5 4 3 2 1

COVER: EZEKIEL ELLIOTT
PAGE 2: LEIGHTON VANDER ESCH
PAGES 6-7: DAK PRESCOTT AND ZACK MARTIN

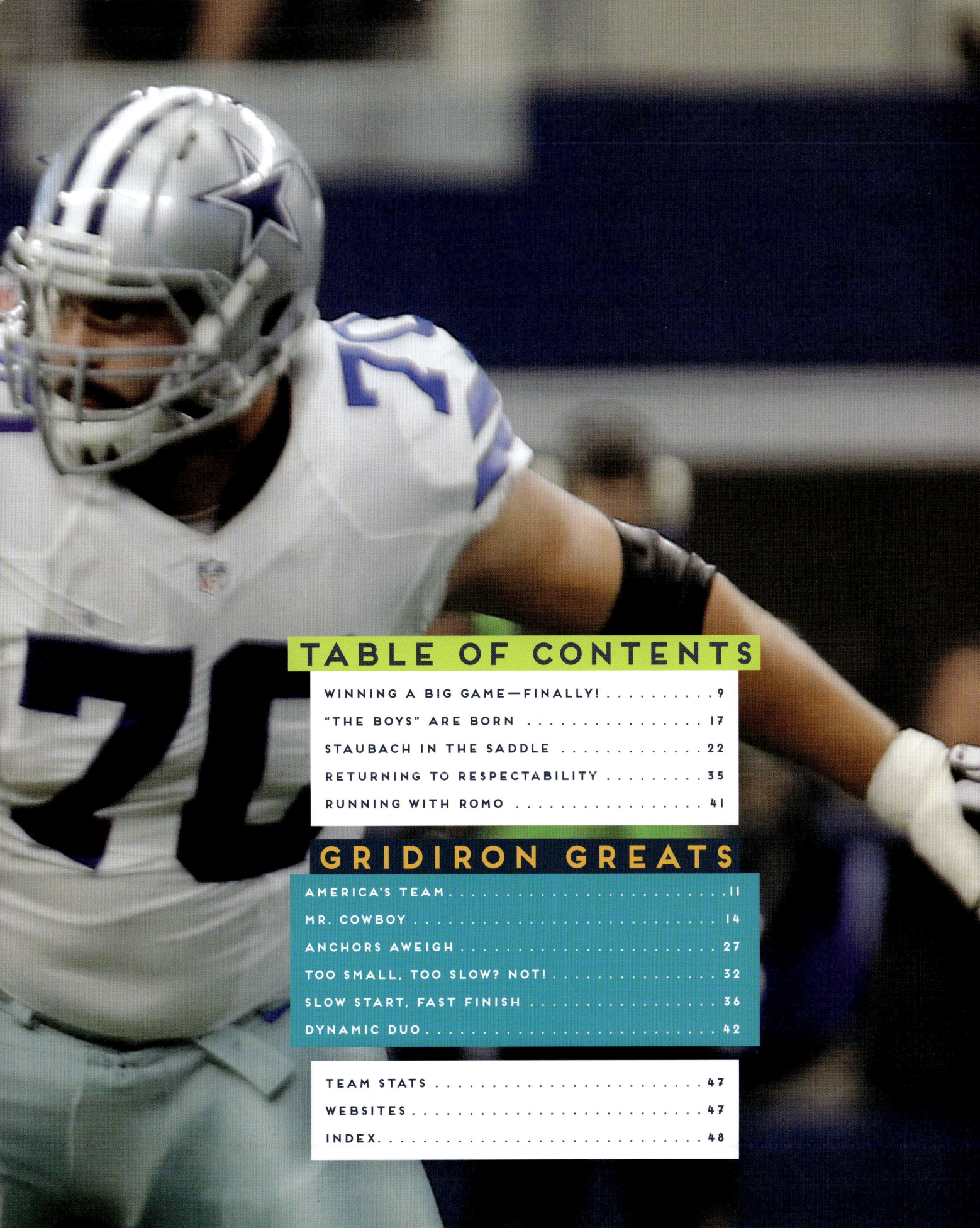

TABLE OF CONTENTS

WINNING A BIG GAME—FINALLY!	9
"THE BOYS" ARE BORN	17
STAUBACH IN THE SADDLE	22
RETURNING TO RESPECTABILITY	35
RUNNING WITH ROMO	41

GRIDIRON GREATS

AMERICA'S TEAM	11
MR. COWBOY	14
ANCHORS AWEIGH	27
TOO SMALL, TOO SLOW? NOT!	32
SLOW START, FAST FINISH	36
DYNAMIC DUO	42

TEAM STATS	47
WEBSITES	47
INDEX	48

RUNNING BACK DUANE THOMAS

WINNING A BIG GAME—FINALLY!

By 1971, many fans thought of the Dallas Cowboys as one of best teams in the National Football League (NFL). From 1966 to 1969, they won the NFL's Capitol Division every year. In 1970, the NFL merged with the American Football League (AFL). The Cowboys kept winning. They won the Eastern Division of the National Football Conference (NFC). During this five-year period, they won 52 games while losing just 16. They were in the playoffs every year.

But some people doubted whether Dallas could win big games. The Cowboys lost the 1966 and 1967 NFL Championship Games. That kept

DALLAS COWBOYS

LEFT: DEFENSIVE TACKLE JETHRO PUGH AND DEFENSIVE END LARRY COLE

them out of the Super Bowl. Three years later, they finally overcame that hurdle. They played in Super Bowl V against the Baltimore Colts. It was one of the sloppiest games ever. The teams combined for 11 turnovers. Dallas blew a seven-point lead early in the fourth quarter. It lost on a last-second field goal. "Next year's champions" became the team's unofficial nickname. It wasn't meant as a compliment.

Halfway through the 1971 season, Dallas was just 4–3. The team had been alternating Craig Morton and Roger Staubach at quarterback. Coach Tom Landry decided to stick with Staubach. It was a great move. The Cowboys won all seven of their remaining games. They rode their defense through the playoffs. They were back in the Super Bowl. They faced the mighty Miami Dolphins. (The next year, the Dolphins would become the first NFL team to go undefeated.)

Team official Gil Brandt knew his team had one big advantage. "I think the thing that helped us the most was the fact that we had been to the Super Bowl the year

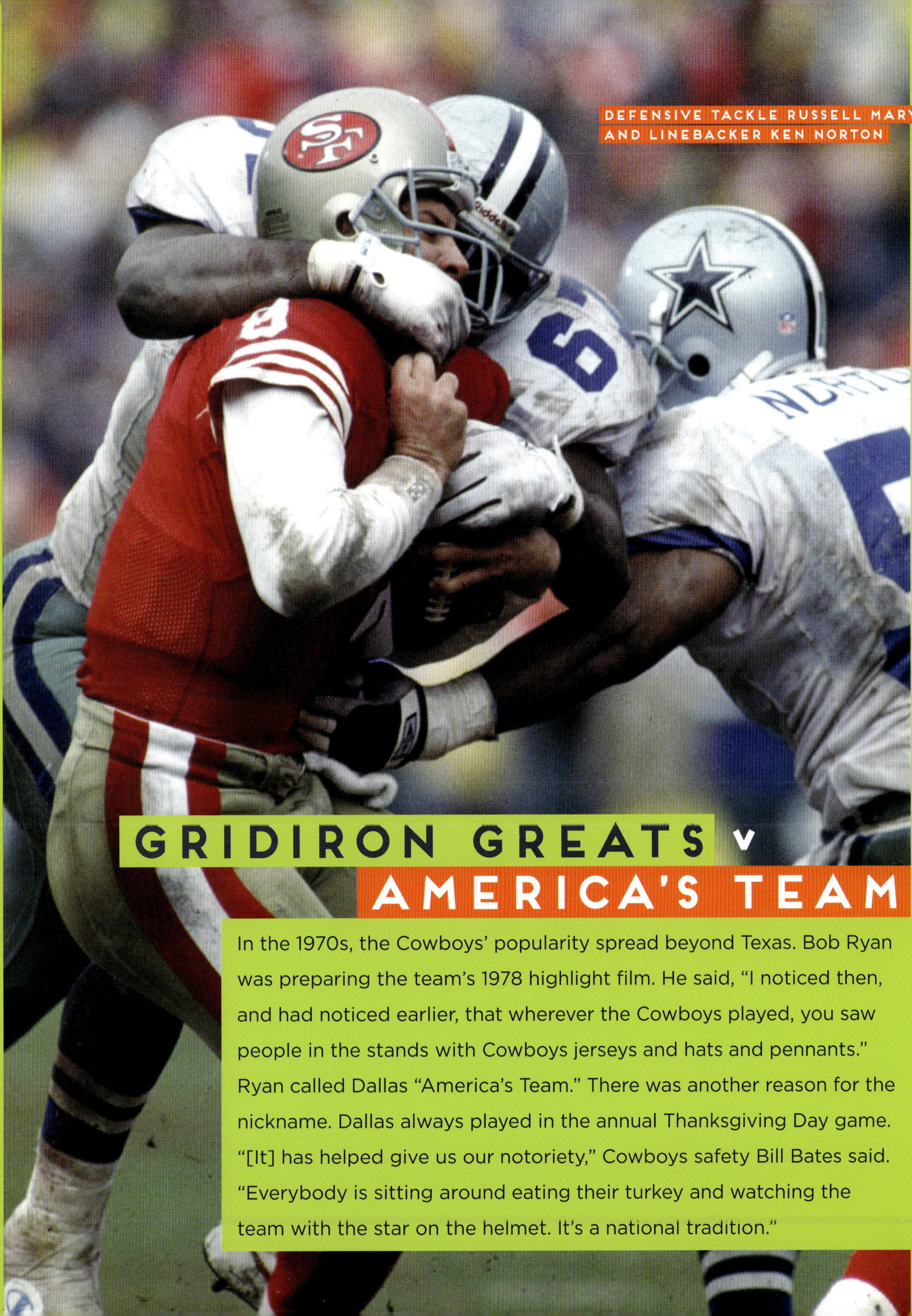

DEFENSIVE TACKLE RUSSELL MARYLAND AND LINEBACKER KEN NORTON

GRIDIRON GREATS v
AMERICA'S TEAM

In the 1970s, the Cowboys' popularity spread beyond Texas. Bob Ryan was preparing the team's 1978 highlight film. He said, "I noticed then, and had noticed earlier, that wherever the Cowboys played, you saw people in the stands with Cowboys jerseys and hats and pennants." Ryan called Dallas "America's Team." There was another reason for the nickname. Dallas always played in the annual Thanksgiving Day game. "[It] has helped give us our notoriety," Cowboys safety Bill Bates said. "Everybody is sitting around eating their turkey and watching the team with the star on the helmet. It's a national tradition."

DALLAS COWBOYS

LINEBACKER DAVE EDWARDS AND LARRY COLE

"WHEN WE WON SUPER BOWL VI, WE FINALLY FELT LIKE WE'D GOTTEN IT DONE."

—GIL BRANDT

before," he said. "So all the issues facing first-timers—nerves, logistics—were less of a problem." Defensive tackle Bob Lilly set the tone early in the game. He sacked Dolphins quarterback Bob Griese for a 29-yard loss. That is still the biggest loss in Super Bowl history. The Dallas defense shut down Miami. Staubach threw two touchdown passes. Running back Duane Thomas rushed for 95 yards. That was more than the entire Miami team. Dallas steamrolled Miami, 24–3. The decisive victory ended all talk of Dallas being "second-best." "It felt like the load of the world was taken off our backs," Brandt said. "When we won Super Bowl VI, we finally felt like we'd gotten it done." Since then, the Cowboys have "gotten it done" many times. They've returned to the Super Bowl on numerous occasions.

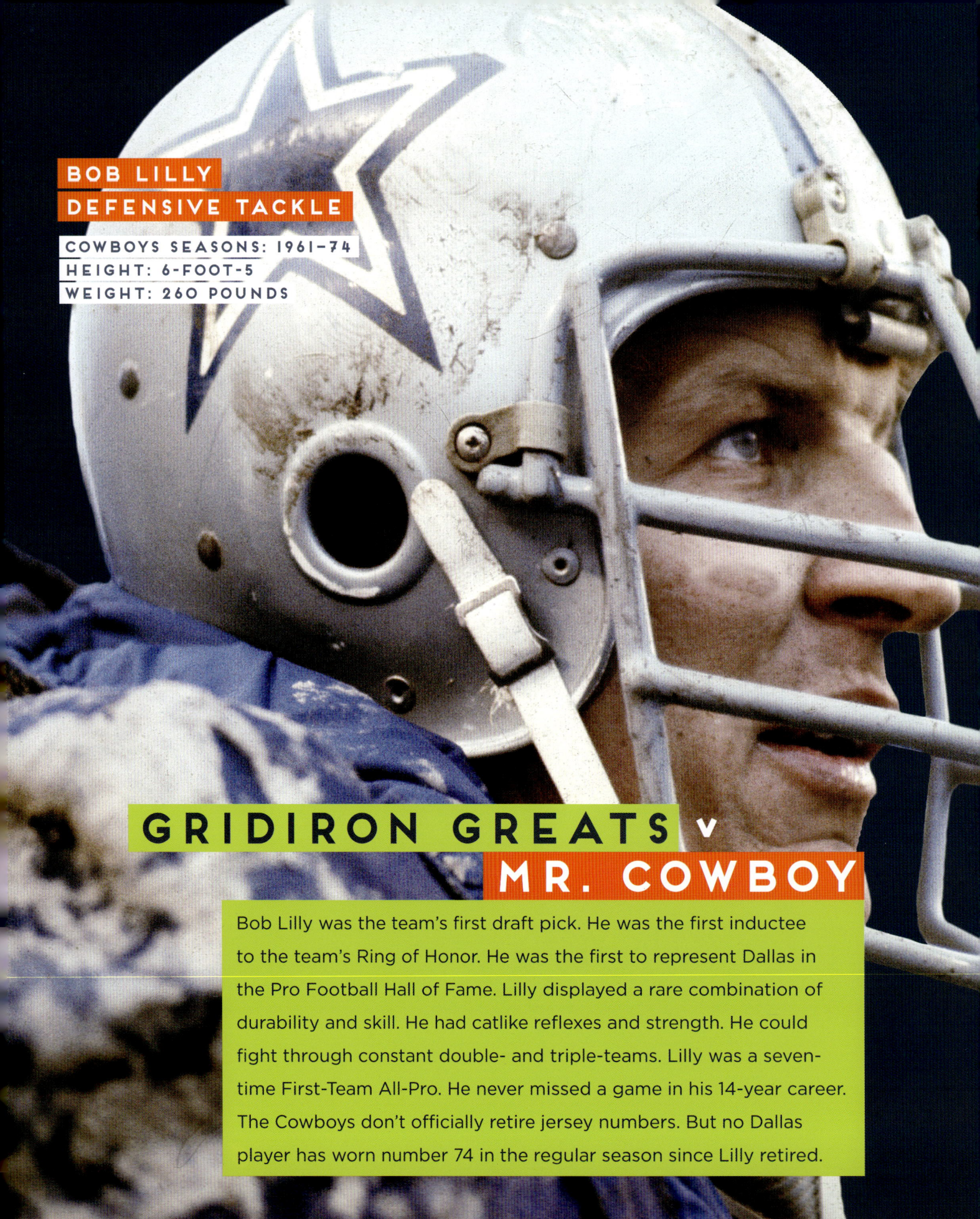

BOB LILLY
DEFENSIVE TACKLE

COWBOYS SEASONS: 1961–74
HEIGHT: 6-FOOT-5
WEIGHT: 260 POUNDS

GRIDIRON GREATS v
MR. COWBOY

Bob Lilly was the team's first draft pick. He was the first inductee to the team's Ring of Honor. He was the first to represent Dallas in the Pro Football Hall of Fame. Lilly displayed a rare combination of durability and skill. He had catlike reflexes and strength. He could fight through constant double- and triple-teams. Lilly was a seven-time First-Team All-Pro. He never missed a game in his 14-year career. The Cowboys don't officially retire jersey numbers. But no Dallas player has worn number 74 in the regular season since Lilly retired.

1960 DALLAS TEXANS GAME

"THE BOYS" ARE BORN

The Dallas Cowboys were born out of a rivalry. Millionaire Lamar Hunt wanted to bring an NFL team to Dallas. The league turned him down. So he started his own league. In 1959, he joined forces with seven other men. The group established the AFL. Hunt's team would be named the Dallas Texans. That got the NFL's attention. To compete with the AFL, the NFL awarded an expansion team to Dallas millionaire Clint Murchison Jr. He hired Tex Schramm as general manager. Schramm set up his office in

a corner of the Texas Auto Club. "People would crowd in there to map routes for trips, and I'd be over in a corner discussing player contracts on the phone," Schramm remembered. "Sometimes they'd listen in. The noise was unbelievable."

Murchison and Schramm knew who they wanted as coach: Tom Landry. He was a Texas native and the New York Giants' defensive coordinator. "People were calling him a young genius for what he had done with the Giants' defense," Schramm later said. At quarterback, Schramm wanted All-American "Dandy Don" Meredith. Schramm asked his friend George Halas, owner of the Chicago Bears, for help. Halas took Meredith in the 1960 NFL Draft. Then he traded Meredith to Dallas. Schramm used a similar tactic to get running back Don Perkins.

Most of the rest of the team was drawn from a pool of other teams' players. Dallas wasn't very good. It finished its first season without a win. The Cowboys won four games the next year. They improved to five wins in 1962. Competition for fans forced Hunt to move the Texans in 1963. Dallas now belonged solely to the Cowboys. And the Cowboys' offense now belonged to Meredith. He and Perkins led the offensive charge. Bob Lilly led the defense. Dallas had selected Lilly with its first-ever draft pick in 1961. The Cowboys then added linebacker Lee Roy

DON MEREDITH AND TOM LANDRY

> "PEOPLE WERE CALLING HIM A YOUNG GENIUS FOR WHAT HE HAD DONE WITH THE GIANTS' DEFENSE."
> —TEX SCHRAMM ON TOM LANDRY

Jordan. Ballhawking safety Mel Renfro and the world-class sprinter of a wide receiver Bob Hayes arrived in 1964. Hayes would become the only athlete to win both an Olympic gold medal and a Super Bowl ring.

In 1966, Dallas made the playoffs for the first time. But the Green Bay Packers stopped them in the NFL Championship. The teams faced off again for the 1967 championship. The Cowboys traveled to wintry Wisconsin. The official game-time temperature was -13 °F (-25 °C). Factoring in wind chill, it was -23 °F (-30.6 °C). The field froze into a sheet of ice. The conditions led to the game's "Ice Bowl" nickname. The Packers scored a touchdown with just 13 seconds left. Dallas was left with a bitter 21–17 defeat. "I was just happy to get out of that game alive," Lilly said. "I'll never forget that game."

DON MEREDITH IN THE "ICE BOWL"

STAUBACH IN THE SADDLE

BOB HAYES

The Cowboys continued to top their division for the next four years. They lost in the playoffs to the Cleveland Browns in 1968 and 1969. Then, in 1970, the Cowboys rolled all the way to Super Bowl V. Baltimore won on a late field goal in what became known as the "Blunder Bowl." Dallas linebacker Chuck Howley was named the game's Most Valuable Player (MVP). It was the first time a player of the losing team earned the honor.

DALLAS COWBOYS

ROGER STAUBACH

The Cowboys needed a spark. It came in the form of Roger Staubach. He was nicknamed "Roger the Dodger." He was good at slipping away from opposing tacklers. Staubach marched Dallas to Super Bowl VI. The team's defense limited Miami to just 185 yards of total offense. The Cowboys won, 24–3. After more than a decade of close calls, Dallas finally had its first title. Staubach claimed Super Bowl MVP honors. "My most satisfying moment as a professional was in that locker room," Staubach later said. "I looked around that locker room at Bob Lilly, Chuck Howley, and the other veterans. I could see the pride on their faces. It was a great feeling."

DALLAS COWBOYS

153
153 CAREER PASSING TOUCHDOWNS

131
131 GAMES PLAYED

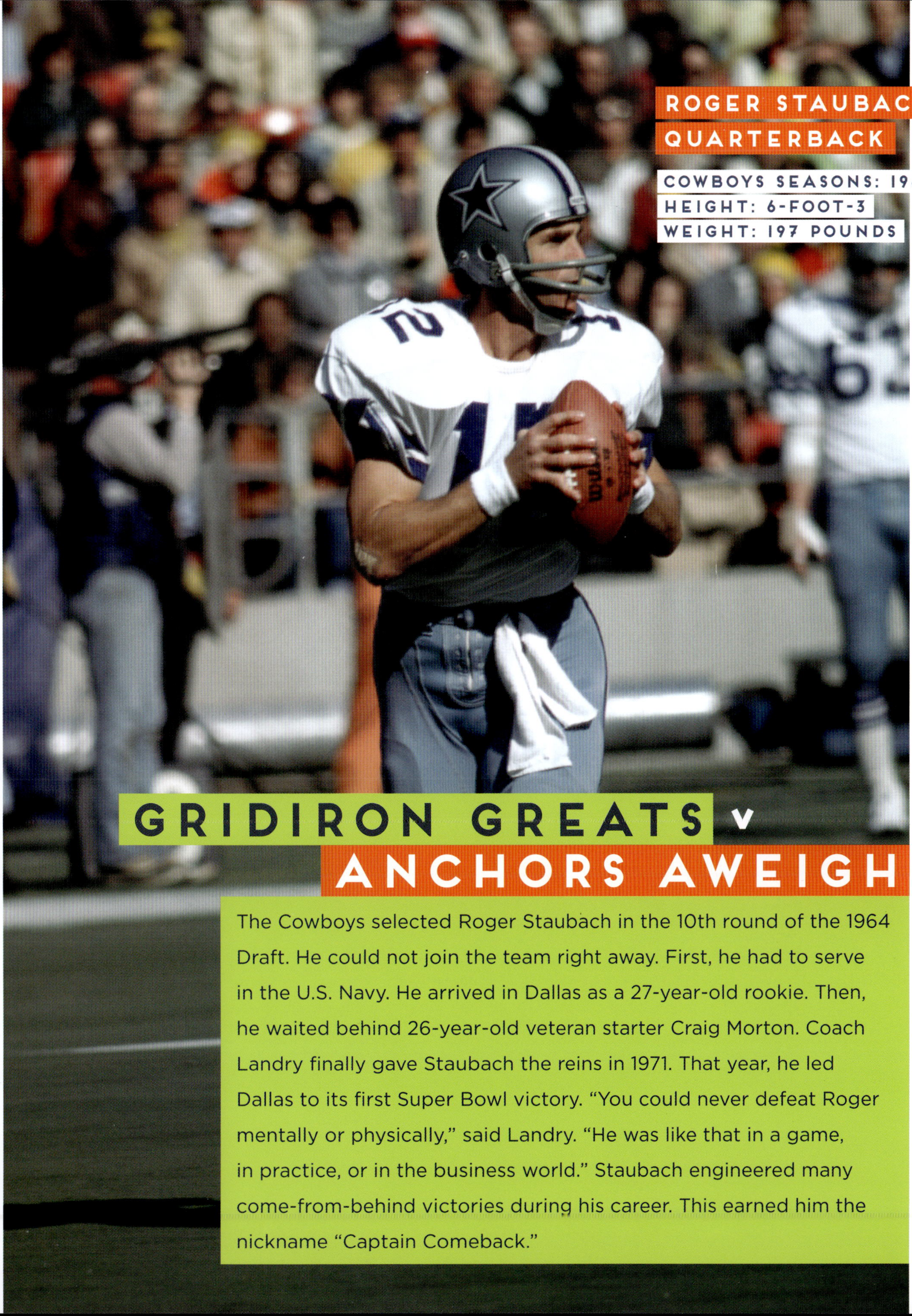

ROGER STAUBACH
QUARTERBACK

COWBOYS SEASONS: 1969–79
HEIGHT: 6-FOOT-3
WEIGHT: 197 POUNDS

GRIDIRON GREATS v
ANCHORS AWEIGH

The Cowboys selected Roger Staubach in the 10th round of the 1964 Draft. He could not join the team right away. First, he had to serve in the U.S. Navy. He arrived in Dallas as a 27-year-old rookie. Then, he waited behind 26-year-old veteran starter Craig Morton. Coach Landry finally gave Staubach the reins in 1971. That year, he led Dallas to its first Super Bowl victory. "You could never defeat Roger mentally or physically," said Landry. "He was like that in a game, in practice, or in the business world." Staubach engineered many come-from-behind victories during his career. This earned him the nickname "Captain Comeback."

DALLAS COWBOYS

WIDE RECEIVER DREW PEARSON

Dallas enjoyed back-to-back 10–4 records. But both years ended in NFC Championship Game losses. The 1974 season marked the first time in nearly a decade that Dallas did not make the postseason. In 1975, the Cowboys charged back to the Super Bowl. The game went down to the wire. But Dallas lost, 21–17, to the Pittsburgh Steelers. Two years later, a new star arrived: running back Tony Dorsett. He racked up 13 touchdowns and rushed for

TONY DORSETT

DEFENSIVE END ED "TOO TALL" JONES

1,007 yards. The Cowboys galloped back to the top of the NFC East Division. Dorsett earned the Offensive Rookie of the Year award. The Cowboys compiled a 12–2 record. They gave up just 13 total points in the playoffs. They cruised into Super Bowl XII. Their defense was strong. It forced the Denver Broncos to cough up eight turnovers. Dallas won, 27–10.

Dallas enjoyed another great season in 1978. The Cowboys faced the Steelers in Super Bowl XIII. But they lost. In each of the next five years, Dallas was bounced from the playoffs. It was clear that the team's supremacy was declining. In 1983, a number of Dallas greats retired. From 1986 to 1990, the once-mighty "Boys" posted losing records. They hit rock bottom in 1989. They won just one game.

EMMITT SMITH
RUNNING BACK

COWBOYS SEASONS: 1990–2002
HEIGHT: 5-FOOT-9
WEIGHT: 221 POUNDS

GRIDIRON GREATS

TOO SMALL, TOO SLOW? NOT!

Many people thought Emmitt Smith was too small and too slow to excel in the NFL. But Smith had other strengths. He was smart, agile, and powerful. He utilized an explosive burst to hit every hole hard. He even distracted his teammates. "One of the biggest mistakes I used to make was just watching him after I handed him the ball, instead of continuing the fake," said quarterback Troy Aikman. Smith became only the fourth player to win three straight NFL rushing titles. When he left the Cowboys, he was the league's all-time rushing leader.

175

175 CAREER TOUCHDOWNS

226

226 GAMES PLAYED

WIDE RECEIVER MICHAEL IRVIN

RETURNING TO RESPECTABILITY

Businessman Jerry Jones bought the team in 1989. He was determined to turn the franchise around. One of his first moves was firing Landry. Landry had been Dallas's only head coach. The team began laying the foundation for a return to greatness. It drafted savvy young quarterback Troy Aikman first overall in 1989. Hard-nosed running back Emmitt Smith arrived the following year. Smith was smaller than most NFL players. This caused some to doubt that he would succeed. But he quickly dispelled those doubts. He rolled up 1,165 total yards and 11 touchdowns in his first season. He earned Offensive Rookie of the Year honors. "Sixteen teams passed on me [in the draft]," he said. "I was beginning to

GRIDIRON GREATS
SLOW START, FAST FINISH

Troy Aikman was the first overall selection in the 1989 Draft. But his first season was terrible. Dallas lost every game he started. After three years, things changed. He led the Cowboys to a 52-17 victory in Super Bowl XXVII. He was the game's MVP. When he retired, he was only the third quarterback in NFL history to lead his team to three Super Bowl victories. "In my opinion, he's fundamentally the best quarterback that's ever played the game," said Tampa Bay Buccaneer Trent Dilfer. "You cannot find a flaw in his mechanics drop, his throwing motion, balance, all that stuff."

TROY AIKMAN
QUARTERBACK

COWBOYS SEASONS: 1989–2000
HEIGHT: 6-FOOT-4
WEIGHT: 219 POUNDS

LEFT: RUNNING BACK HERSCHEL WALKER

think I wouldn't go until the second round. But I hope 16 teams are kicking themselves now."

Aikman, Smith, and wide receiver Michael Irvin were nicknamed "The Triplets." In 1992, they accounted for more than 6,500 total yards of offense. The Cowboys went 13–3. They barreled through the playoffs. They met the Buffalo Bills in Super Bowl XXVII. Aikman threw four touchdown passes. The Cowboys crushed the Bills, 52–17. It was their third Super Bowl title. Dallas returned to the big game the following season. It faced the Bills again. This time, Smith was the star. He ran for 132 yards and 2 touchdowns to lead his team to a 30–13 victory. In 1994, San Francisco dashed Dallas's hopes for a three-peat. The 49ers defeated the Cowboys in the NFC Championship Game. By then, the Cowboys had padded their roster with another weapon: Deion Sanders. He was a speedy cornerback and kick returner.

The 1995 Cowboys reached Super Bowl XXX. They met Pittsburgh, their old nemesis. The Steelers had beaten Dallas in two previous Super Bowls. Dallas got some payback. The Cowboys pulled out a 27–17 victory. It was their third title in four years. Tackle Chad Hennings had two sacks. Cornerback Larry Brown grabbed two interceptions. "Every time somebody counted us out, I looked to my right and looked to my left. I saw my boys right and left, and we squeezed a little bit tighter," Irvin said. "The bottom line is that we got it done."

The Cowboys made the playoffs three more times in the late 1990s. But with each passing season, they grew weaker. Then they missed the playoffs for three years. Smith remained a steady presence in Dallas. In 2002, he surpassed former Chicago Bears great Walter Payton as the NFL's all-time rushing leader. In 2003, the Cowboys returned to the playoffs. The Carolina Panthers eliminated them in the Wild Card round. But hope for the future had been restored.

TROY AIKMAN

TONY ROMO

RUNNING WITH ROMO

During the next two years, the Cowboys fell short of the postseason. Midway through 2006, Tony Romo took the reins. He had joined Dallas as an undrafted free agent two years earlier. He began his career as a placekick holder. Now the starting quarterback, he made an immediate impact. He threw 19 touchdown passes and racked up nearly 3,000 yards. Dallas returned to the playoffs in the Wild Card game. It was in position to defeat the Seattle Seahawks. The Cowboys set up a field goal in the game's final moments. But Romo botched the snap. Seattle escaped with a 21–20 win.

The Cowboys won 13 games the following year. The offense put plenty of points on the scoreboard. The solid defense was led by

DALLAS COWBOYS

EZEKIEL ELLIOTT
RUNNING BACK

COWBOYS SEASONS: 2016–PRESENT
HEIGHT: 6 FEET
WEIGHT: 228 POUNDS

DAK PRESCOTT
QUARTERBACK

COWBOYS SEASONS: 2016–PRESENT
HEIGHT: 6-FOOT-2
WEIGHT: 238 POUNDS

GRIDIRON GREATS
DYNAMIC DUO

It was obvious that a Dallas player would be 2016 Offensive Rookie of the Year. Running back Ezekiel Elliott piled up 1,631 rushing yards. He topped the league. He was the first rookie in 17 years to do so. Quarterback Dak Prescott passed for 3,667 yards and 23 touchdowns. Both players were named to the Pro Bowl. It was the first time that a rookie running back and quarterback from the same team had been selected. The voters had a difficult choice. Twenty-eight picked Prescott. Elliott had 21 votes. "Do we have a knife to cut this [the trophy] in half?" Prescott said. "He [Elliott] deserves it just as much as I do."

311

311 COMPLETED PASSES IN 2016 - PRESCOTT

322

322 RUSHING ATTEMPTS IN 2016 - ELLIOTT

LEFT: WIDE RECEIVER DEZ BRYANT

rising star DeMarcus Ware, a pass-rushing linebacker. Unfortunately, Dallas again suffered a bitter first-round playoff loss. Many experts considered the 2008 Cowboys to have the most talented roster in the NFC. But they struggled after Romo was sidelined with a broken finger. Dallas finished 9–7.

In 2009, the team moved to the new Cowboys Stadium. The change of scenery was just what it needed. The Cowboys put together an 11–5 record. They topped the NFC East. They hosted the Philadelphia Eagles in the first round of the playoffs. For the first time since 1996, Dallas won a playoff matchup. Then its luck ran out. The Minnesota Vikings pummeled the Cowboys in the divisional round, 34–3. They started poorly in 2010. In Week 7, things got worse. Romo suffered a broken collarbone. Any hopes for playing in the postseason faded.

After Romo recovered, he helped the Cowboys improve to 8–8 in 2011. Dallas repeated that record in the next two seasons. The 2014 season began with a loss to the 49ers. Many people thought it would be yet another bad year. But the team came around. Romo had the league's highest pass completion rating. The Boys finished 12–4. Running back DeMarco Murray led the league in rushing. He was named Offensive Player of the Year. The Cowboys posted a win over the Detroit Lions in the Wild Card. But then they fell to the Packers.

DEMARCO MURRAY

LINEBACKER JAYLON SMITH (NUMBER 54)

Both Romo and wide receiver Dez Bryant were injured early in 2015. The Cowboys finished 4–12. It was their worst record since 1989. But they hit paydirt in the 2016 Draft. They selected running back Ezekiel Elliott and quarterback Dak Prescott. The pair powered Dallas to tie the team's best-ever record of 13–3. Prescott edged out Elliott for Offensive Rookie of the Year. Unfortunately, the Cowboys lost to Green Bay in the playoffs, 34–31. In 2018, the Cowboys finished 10–6. They beat the Seahawks in the Wild Card. The Los Angeles Rams knocked them out the following week, though.

The Dallas Cowboys and their fans have enjoyed many long rides to the playoffs and beyond during their long history in the NFL. They've already ridden to more than 30 playoff appearances and returned home with 5 Super Bowl championships. Now a new generation is eager to see the Cowboys crowned football's champions once again.

TEAM STATS

NFL CHAMPIONSHIPS

1971, 1977, 1992, 1993, 1995

WEBSITES

DALLAS COWBOYS
https://www.dallascowboys.com/

NFL: DALLAS COWBOYS TEAM PAGE
http://www.nfl.com/teams/dallascowboys/profile?team=DAL

DALLAS COWBOYS

INDEX

DALLAS COWBOYS

AFL/NFL merger 9
Aikman, Troy 32, 35, 36, 38
Bates, Bill 11
"Blunder Bowl" 22
Brandt, Gil 10, 13
Brown, Larry 38
Bryant, Dez 46
Cowboys Stadium 44
division championships 9, 22, 30, 44
Dorsett, Tony 29, 30
Elliott, Ezekiel 42, 46

Hayes, Bob 20
Hennings, Chad 38
Howley, Chuck 22, 24
"Ice Bowl" 20
Irvin, Michael 38
Jones, Jerry 35
Jordan, Lee Roy 19–20
Landry, Tom 10, 19, 27, 35
Lilly, Bob 13, 14, 19, 20, 24
Meredith, Don 19
Morton, Craig 10, 27
Murchison, Clint, Jr. 17, 19

Murray, DeMarco 44
NFC Championship Game 29, 38
NFL Draft 14, 19, 27, 35, 36, 46
NFL records 39
Offensive Player of the Year 44
Offensive Rookie of the Year 30, 35, 42, 46
Perkins, Don 19
playoffs 9, 10, 20, 22, 30, 38, 39, 41, 44, 46
Prescott, Dak 42, 46
Pro Football Hall of Fame 14
Renfro, Mel 20
Romo, Tony 41, 44, 46
Sanders, Deion 38
Schramm, Tex 17, 19
Smith, Emmitt 32, 35, 38, 39
Staubach, Roger 10, 13, 24, 27
Super Bowl 10, 13, 20, 22, 24, 27, 29, 30, 36, 38, 46
MVP award 22, 24, 36
Thomas, Duane 13
"The Triplets" 38
Ware, DeMarcus 44

TIGHT END JASON WITTEN

48